Essential Life Science

VARIATION AND CLASSIFICATION

Melanie Waldron

Heinemann
LIBRARY

Chicago, Illinois

© 2014 Heinemann Library
an imprint of Capstone Global Library, LLC
Chicago, Illinois

To contact Capstone Global Library, please
call 800-747-4992, or visit our web site,
www.capstonepub.com

Edited by Andrew Farrow and Diyan Leake
Designed by Victoria Allen
Original illustrations © Capstone Global
    Library Ltd 2014
Picture research by Ruth Blair
Production by Sophia Argyris
Originated by Capstone Global Library Ltd
Printed in China by CTPS

17 16 15 14 13
10 9 8 7 6 5 4 3 2

Library of Congress Cataloging-in-Publication Data
Waldron, Melanie.
  Variation and classification / Melanie Waldron.
      pages cm—(Essential life science)
  Includes bibliographical references and index.
  ISBN 9781432978136 (hb) ISBN 9781432978440 (pb) 1.
Plants—Classification—Juvenile literature.
I. Title.
  QK49 .W1455 2014
  581—dc23   2012051619

Acknowledgments
We would like to thank the following for permission
to reproduce photographs: Alamy pp. 5 (© Corbis
Flirt), 18 (© Vincent MacNamara), 26 (© blickwinkel),
37 (© Frans Lemmens; Capstone Publishers (© Karon
Dubke) pp. 8, 9, 21, 24, 25, 40, 41); Corbis p. 14 (© Flip
Nicklin/Minden Pictures); © Andre Engels p. 36; FLPA
p. 43 (Eric Woods); Getty Images pp. 4 (Alexander
Safonov), 10 (Rebekka Gudleifsdottir), 13 (Beverly
Joubert), 19 (Martin Harvey), 35 (Sylvain Cordier),
42 (Nigel Cattlin); Shutterstock pp. 16 (© cosma), 22
(© Rob kemp), 28 (© RomGams), 30 (© Vlad61), 31
(© Harald Toepfer), 34 (© Richard Whitcombe), 38
(© Jacek Chabraszewski); Superstock pp. 6 (Antoine
Juliette/Oredia/Oredia Eurl), 11 (age fotostock), 12
(Minden Pictures), 20 (Cultura Limited), 29 (Minden
Pictures), 32 (Minden Pictures).

Cover photograph of tropical fish on a coral
reef reproduced with permission of Corbis
(© Tischenko Irina).

Contents

Eureka moment!

Learn about important discoveries that have brought about further knowledge and understanding.

DID YOU KNOW?

Discover fascinating facts about variation and classification.

WHAT'S NEXT?

Read about the latest research and advances in essential science.

Some words are shown in bold, **like this**. You can find out what they mean by looking in the glossary.

What Lives on Earth?

How many different types of living thing—both plants and animals—do you think there are on Earth? Would you believe that across the world there are millions of different living things? Each different type of plant or animal is called a **species**. What is even more amazing is that new species are being discovered every year.

Living differences

Everything on Earth is either living or nonliving. To stay alive, all living things need a source of energy, such as food. They also need **oxygen**, found in air and water. Apart from this, there are differences between living things. These differences can be tiny, but they can also be huge.

DID YOU KNOW?

Scientists know about and have named around two million different species of plants and animals. However, some people estimate that there may be between 3 and 100 million species on Earth!

All the living things in this picture need energy and oxygen to stay alive.

Groups of living things

We can look at how living things are different. This is called **variation**. We can try to group similar living things together. This is called **classification**. All living things can be split into five main groups. Animals and plants are the two main groups that this book will focus on. Fungi are a bit like plants and include mushrooms and toadstools. Protists and bacteria make up the last two groups. These tiny, microscopic living things are found all over the world, in the air, soil, and water.

All humans are the same species. But there are differences, or variations, between us all.

What Is Variation?

Variation is how things are different. Just think of all the plants and animals you know, and what makes them different from each other. Animals can have two legs, four legs, or no legs. Some have fur, and some have scales. Some plants have yellow flowers, and some have red flowers.

All of these living things are different because they are different species. However, even things that are the same species can look different. All humans are the same species, but nearly all of us look different. Sometimes twins can look very similar.

All of these children have the same mother and father. Yet they are all different. This is because of variation.

Inherited variations

Some variations—for example, your height or the shape of your earlobes—are inherited. This means that you get these **traits** from your parents. Parents pass on their **genes** to their children. Genes are the pieces of information inside all your body parts that tell your body what to be like. Since you get a mix of your mother's and your father's genes, your traits will be a mix of theirs. This is the same for all animals and plants.

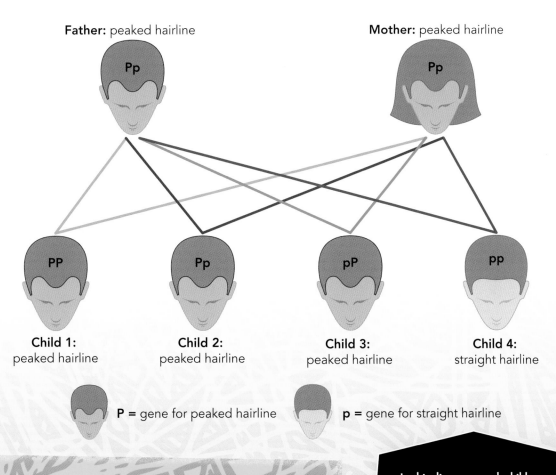

Father: peaked hairline
Pp

Mother: peaked hairline
Pp

PP
Child 1: peaked hairline

Pp
Child 2: peaked hairline

pP
Child 3: peaked hairline

pp
Child 4: straight hairline

P = gene for peaked hairline

p = gene for straight hairline

Eureka moment!

Gregor Mendel was a scientist. In the 1860s, he was the first person to say that the results of his experiments were because of inherited traits. He did not experiment using humans, though—he used pea plants!

In this diagram, each child gets one "hairline" gene from each parent. There can be four combinations, and this will decide what each child's hairline will be like.

Try this!

Continuous variation means that there will be a wide range of differences in one species. You can see this if you look at the height of people within a group, for example.

Prediction

Children of similar ages are not all the same height. Their heights will show a continuous variation.

What you need

- A tape measure
- A height chart
- A pencil
- A piece of paper
- As many students in the same grade at school as possible

What you do

1. Measure the heights of all the students in the grade. Do this by asking them to stand straight, with their backs against the wall, where the height chart is.

2. Write down each student's height on a piece of paper.

3 List all the heights in order, from smallest to tallest. This may be easier to do on a computer, using a spreadsheet.

4 Now plot your results on a bar graph. Put the heights along the horizontal axis, or x-axis. Label the vertical axis, or y-axis, from 0 to 10. If some people are the same height, make the bar taller, depending on how many people are that height.

Conclusion

Your results will show that there is a range of heights, from the smallest to the tallest. This is because height is a continuous variation. Most people will be toward the middle of the range. Does your bar graph show this?

Different variations

Plants and animals of the same species can be different because of the **environment** they live in. For example, hydrangeas are plants with big flowers. The color of the flowers depends on the type of soil the plant is growing in. Horses living in cold countries will grow much thicker coats than horses living in hot countries.

Learning differently

Many animals can learn different things. For example, sea otters can learn to break open shells using stones. People can learn to speak different languages. You can learn to ski, write, or ride a bicycle. These are all learned traits—you do not inherit them from your parents' genes.

These Icelandic horses grow long, thick coats to cope with the cold conditions in Iceland.

Different behaviors

Plants and animals in different **habitats** and environments can behave differently. For example, springtime daffodils growing in some southern parts of the United States will often bloom sooner than those farther north. This is because they respond to warm temperatures, and southern areas are usually warmer earlier in the year than northern areas.

Crops that are sprayed with pesticides and fertilizers and watered in dry weather will grow much better than the same plants in the wild.

Natural selection

Sometimes plants or animals have variations that make them better suited to their environment than others. For example, imagine two stick insects, each a slightly different shade of green. One shade of green might blend in better with the plants they live on. This would mean that the other one would be slightly easier to spot among the plants and would therefore be the first to get eaten by **predators**.

The insect with better camouflage would live longer, and so would be able to have more **offspring**. Eventually, all the less well camouflaged stick insects would die out. This process is called **natural selection**.

When this leafy sea dragon is hiding among seaweed, it is difficult for predators to spot it, and so it avoids being eaten.

The fittest

Natural selection means that variations will give some plants and animals a better chance of survival than others. They will live longer and will have more offspring. This is also called survival of the fittest.

Over a long period of time, with natural selection, plants and animals can gradually change so that they become best suited to their environment. This means that different environments will have different plants and animals living there.

The lion might catch the slowest gazelle, while the faster ones might escape and go on to have fast offspring.

Eureka moment!

In 1832, Charles Darwin set sail on a voyage of discovery. Over the next few years, he discovered that animals living on the Galapagos Islands, off the South American coast, were slightly different than the similar animals on the mainland. He suggested natural selection to explain these differences.

What Is Evolution?

Evolution is the name given to the very slow process, over thousands of years, in which plants and animals change to become more and more different from each other. Eventually, they change so much that they become different species.

Evolution begins with natural selection. Plants or animals with traits best suited to their environments will survive better. These traits will be passed on to their offspring in the genes from the parents. This happens again and again, with tiny differences in traits passing down from parent to offspring, then to their offspring, and so on. Over a long period of time, all these tiny differences will add up to a large difference, and the result will be that a new species has evolved.

Millions of years ago, some land-living animals moved into water to find food and cool down. Over time, they evolved into new species, like this blue whale.

Evolving bears

Polar bears are a different species than brown bears. Scientists think that this split first happened about 500,000 years ago. Brown bears living around the Arctic gradually evolved over time and became a new species—polar bears—that was far better suited to living in snowy conditions than brown bears.

DID YOU KNOW?

Human beings evolved from animals, a bit like chimpanzees, that moved around on all fours. Between four and six million years ago, early humans started to walk upright on two legs. Some scientists think this was because it made it easier for them to carry around precious things, such as food.

Polar bear

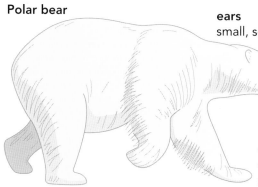

ears
small, so they don't lose heat

fur
colorless hair that looks white, skin underneath is black

head/neck
long and narrow, to move easily through water

feet
wide, with tiny bumps underneath to grip ice, and some webbing between toes to help when swimming

upright height (male): 7–11 feet (2–3.4 meters)
weight (male): 660–1,320 pounds (330–600 kilograms)

Brown bear

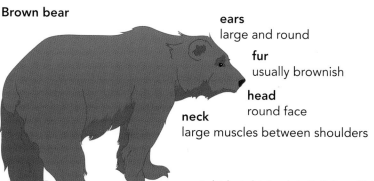

ears
large and round

fur
usually brownish

head
round face

neck
large muscles between shoulders

upright height (male): 5–9 feet (1.5–2.7 meters)
weight (male): 400–1,700 pounds (180–770 kilograms)

Polar bears and brown bears are different in many ways.

How do we know about evolution?

Fossils show us that plants and animals have evolved and changed over time. They are the remains of plants and animals that lived hundreds of thousands of years ago. They are different than the plants and animals alive today. Scientists can figure out how old fossils are, so we know which ones were alive at different times throughout Earth's history. Today's elephants are part of a group called Proboscidea. There are fossils of animals that are also in the Proboscidea group. The name means that they have trunks.

This is a fossil of a type of lizard that lived long ago.

Extinction

At some times in Earth's history, the environment changed a lot over a short period of time. This led to many species becoming **extinct**, because they could not evolve in time to cope with the changes.

For example, around 65 million years ago, dinosaurs existed. Then something disastrous happened, possibly a huge asteroid hitting Earth. This would have caused the skies to become full of dust and ash. The Sun's light would have been blocked out, and plants would not have been able to grow well. There would have been less food for animals as a result. Also, the dust and ash would have trapped Earth's heat, causing temperatures to soar. However, some living things managed to survive and continued to evolve. These included small, bird-like dinosaurs, shrew-like **mammals**, turtles, snails, and some plants.

WHAT'S NEXT?

There have been five major mass extinctions in Earth's history—when dramatic events have wiped out huge numbers of species. Some people are now worried that human activities may cause the sixth mass extinction.

The mass extinction 65 million years ago killed off most animals and plants.

What Is Classification?

Evolution over millions of years has led to a huge number of species of plants and animals on Earth. To make it easier to understand them and study them, scientists put them into groups so that similar living things are in similar groups. This is called classification. Things in a group have similar traits or **characteristics**.

Different species can belong to the same group, if they have similar characteristics. For example, giraffes, pigs, hippopotamuses, camels, and antelopes are all different species. However, they all have four legs, hooves split into two parts, and tails. They all belong to a group called even-toed ungulates.

Cows and sheep both have hooves split in two, four legs, and a tail. Yet they are clearly different species!

Ancestors

When animals share some characteristics, like the even-toed ungulates, it often means that they have the same **ancestors**. This means that millions of years ago, they evolved from the same animals. Over time, they all developed their own characteristics, making them all different species, but they still share some other characteristics.

Humans and chimpanzees are descended from the same group of animals. Around 7 to 10 million years ago, the group split, and human-like animals started to evolve.

Eureka moment!

In 2002, researchers in Chad in Africa found fossil remains of a very ancient human ancestor. The bones are around six to seven million years old. From studying the bones, scientists think that this early human walked on two legs.

Classification systems

Humans have classified things for thousands of years. Even sorting wild animals into those that might eat you and those that won't is a useful classification! Grouping together plants that are safe to eat, or animals that are easy to hunt, would have helped humans to survive thousands of years ago.

You can classify things in lots of different ways. For example, you could sort animals into groups according to the number of legs they have or their color. However, a **classification system** is only really useful if you want other people to be able to understand and use it, too.

We use classification every day, without really realizing it! This girl is classifying her recycling and making sure it goes into the correct bin.

Latin names

Today, scientists across the world still use a classification system drawn up by a Swedish scientist in the 1700s. The system uses Latin words to name things. This gets around the problem of language in different countries or areas. For example, in the United States we use the name *poppy* for a pretty red flower, but in Spain these flowers are called *amapolas*. This is confusing, but the Latin name for the flower, *Papaver rhoeas*, is the same no matter what country you are in.

Rosa rugosa 'Dart's Dash' Rugosa Rose

The label for this plant shows the Latin name, with two common names underneath.

Sometimes males and females of one species can look very different. The brightly colored bird is a male pheasant. The other is a female pheasant.

What is a species?

A species is a single kind of plant or animal with the same set of characteristics. The main thing that makes something a separate species is that a male and female of one species can come together to have offspring.

Some species—for example, dogs—can be split up into different **breeds**. Breeds are still the same species, so different breeds can still produce offspring. Sometimes people decide which traits they want for their **domestic animals**, such as sheep or cows. They select the male and female with the best traits, and the offspring will also have these traits. This is called selective breeding.

Levels of classification

There are different levels of classification. A very simple classification would be to sort things into living and nonliving groups. Living things can then be split into huge groups called **kingdoms**.

Each kingdom can then be divided into smaller groups called phyla. Phyla can be divided into groups called classes, then into orders, families, **genera**, and eventually species. Every kind of plant or animal can be named as an individual species.

DID YOU KNOW?

Humans belong to the order called Primates. This group also includes lemurs, lorises, tarsiers, monkeys, and apes! In fact, there are over 300 species in this order. All primates have thumbs, which means they can grasp things in their hands. Can you think of any other similarities?

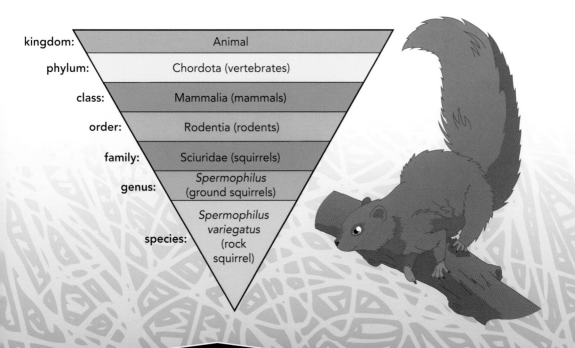

kingdom:	Animal
phylum:	Chordota (vertebrates)
class:	Mammalia (mammals)
order:	Rodentia (rodents)
family:	Sciuridae (squirrels)
genus:	*Spermophilus* (ground squirrels)
species:	*Spermophilus variegatus* (rock squirrel)

This pyramid shows the classification for the rock squirrel. The pyramid narrows as it goes down through the levels. This shows that there are fewer and fewer animals in each level. In the bottom level, there is only one species, the rock squirrel.

Try this!

You can use a classification system to classify many things—not just plants or animals!

Prediction
I can create a classification system for a set of objects. If I explain my classification system, other people will be able to use it to classify the same objects in the same way.

What you need
Any number of different, nonliving items: pen, sock, stone, cotton ball, soft toy, hat, mug, necklace, coin, ball, watch, cushion, phone, spoon, washcloth, glove

What you do

1 Set all of your objects out on a large table.

2 Decide how you might split your objects into groups. You could start by splitting them into two groups: "hard" and "soft." Every time you split groups, remember to write down how you decided to split them.

3 Now look at each group again. How can you split them further? You could split the hard objects into two additional groups: "objects that need power" and "objects that don't need power." How could you split the soft objects?

4 Keep going with each smaller and smaller group of objects. Once you have finished, put the objects back together into one group. Now ask another student to sort the objects, using the groupings you made. Ask him or her to do it in the same order that you did it in.

5 Once your friend has finished, look at the objects. Have they been sorted into the same final groups as when you did the sorting?

Conclusion

If your group descriptions were very clear and careful, other people were able to sort the objects in exactly the same way that you did. Your classification system worked!

How Can Plants Be Classified?

The plant kingdom is one of the five major groups of living things. Plants have some very basic differences from animals. They cannot move around like animals can, and they do not have brains and nerves that control their parts.

The main characteristic of plants is that they can make food for themselves, usually inside their leaves. They do this using the Sun's light, water, and a gas from the air called carbon dioxide. This process of making food is called photosynthesis. Because plants don't need another food source and they produce their own food, they are called producers.

DID YOU KNOW?

Plants growing in rain forests provide us with many things, including timber, coffee, and cocoa. Some of them also contain chemicals that are used to treat diseases such as cancer. Over 2,000 rain forest plants contain anti-cancer chemicals.

Plants create oxygen during photosynthesis. Both plants and animals need oxygen to stay alive.